Wind Chimes and Whirligigs

Renée Schwarz

KIDS CAN PRESS

To Sophie, Pips and Alex — may you find a fair wind …

Kids Can Press acknowledges the financial support of the Government of Ontario, through the Ontario Media Development Corporation's Ontario Book Initiative, and the Government of Canada, through the BPIDP, for our publishing activity.

Published in Canada by
Kids Can Press Ltd.
29 Birch Avenue
Toronto, ON M4V 1E2

Published in the U.S. by
Kids Can Press Ltd.
2250 Military Road
Tonawanda, NY 14150

www.kidscanpress.com

Edited by Stacey Roderick
Designed by Kathleen Collett
Photography by Ray Boudreau

Printed and bound in Singapore

The hardcover edition of this book is smyth sewn casebound.

The paperback edition of this book is limp sewn with a drawn-on cover.

CM 07 0 9 8 7 6 5 4 3 2 1
CM PA 07 0 9 8 7 6 5 4 3 2 1

Library and Archives Canada Cataloguing in Publication

Schwarz, Renée
    Wind chimes and whirligigs / Renée Schwarz.

(Kids can do it)
ISBN-13: 978-1-55337-868-6 (bound)
ISBN-10: 1-55337-868-7 (bound)
ISBN-13: 978-1-55337-870-9 (pbk.)
ISBN-10: 1-55337-870-9 (pbk.)

1. Windchimes — Juvenile literature. 2. Whirligigs — Juvenile literature. 3. Handicraft — Juvenile literature. I. Title. II. Series.

TT157.S36 2007   j745.592   C2006-902601-7

Kids Can Press is a *l'O'r'us*™ Entertainment company

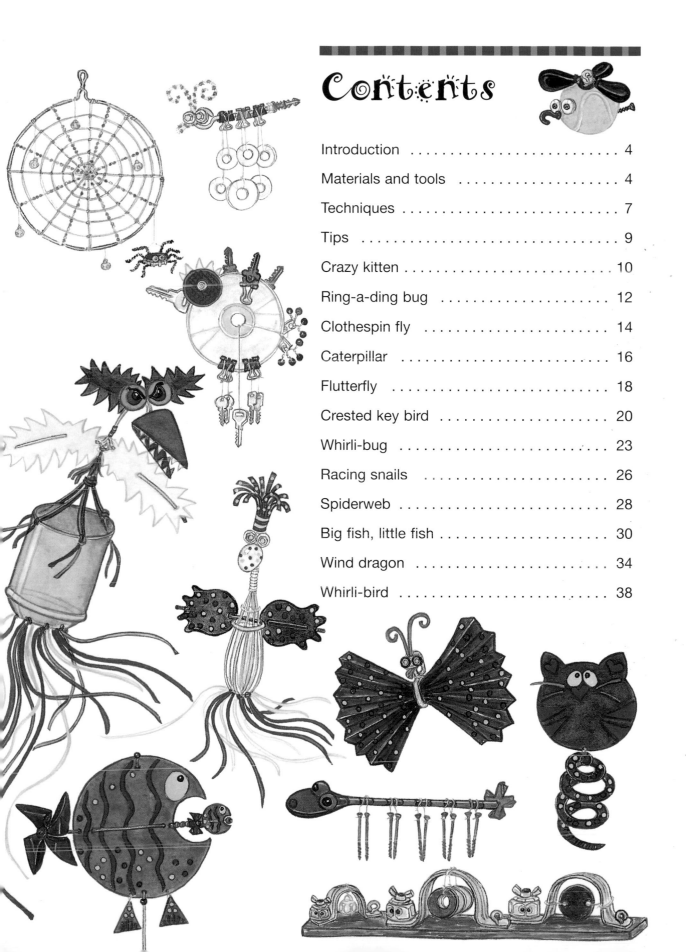

Contents

Introduction 4

Materials and tools 4

Techniques 7

Tips 9

Crazy kitten 10

Ring-a-ding bug 12

Clothespin fly 14

Caterpillar 16

Flutterfly 18

Crested key bird 20

Whirli-bug 23

Racing snails 26

Spiderweb 28

Big fish, little fish 30

Wind dragon 34

Whirli-bird 38

introduction

The fun thing about making wind chimes and whirligigs is hearing them and seeing them dance in the wind. Hang them in your backyard, on the balcony, inside or outside a window or near the door — there are lots of great spots for these wind-powered crafts to catch the wind and fill the air with ringing and whirling.

All the whirligigs in this book can be made into wind chimes just by hanging something that rings from them. And you can add a whirli-thing to all the wind chimes you make. Let your imagination fly!

Materials and tools

You probably already have a lot of the materials and tools you will need. Some will come out of the recycling bin, such as bottles and plastic lids. Ask if you can use washers and screws from the toolbox or old kitchen utensils no one uses. Everything else you'll need can be found in craft stores, hardware stores or dollar stores.

▶ **Some craft and school supplies you'll use**

scissors

hole punch

yellow or light-colored pencils

plastic report covers or sheets of colored acetate

binder clips

pipe cleaners

beads

bells

dowel

nylon ribbon

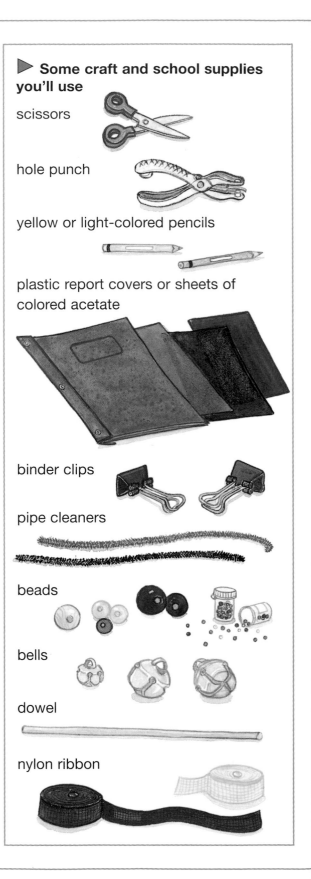

► Other materials you'll need

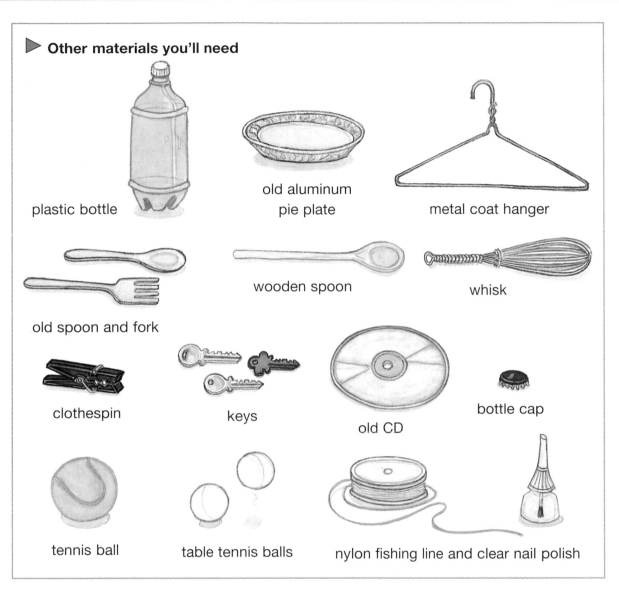

plastic bottle

old aluminum
pie plate

metal coat hanger

wooden spoon

whisk

old spoon and fork

clothespin

keys

old CD

bottle cap

tennis ball

table tennis balls

nylon fishing line and clear nail polish

► For assembling some of the projects, you'll need

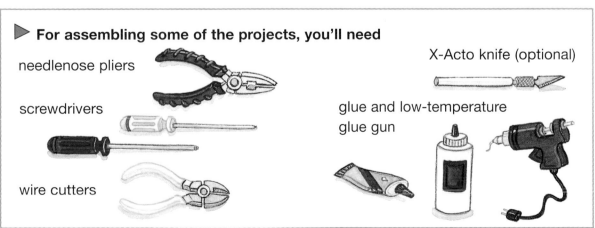

needlenose pliers

screwdrivers

wire cutters

X-Acto knife (optional)

glue and low-temperature
glue gun

5

▶ **Some of the hardware pieces you'll use**

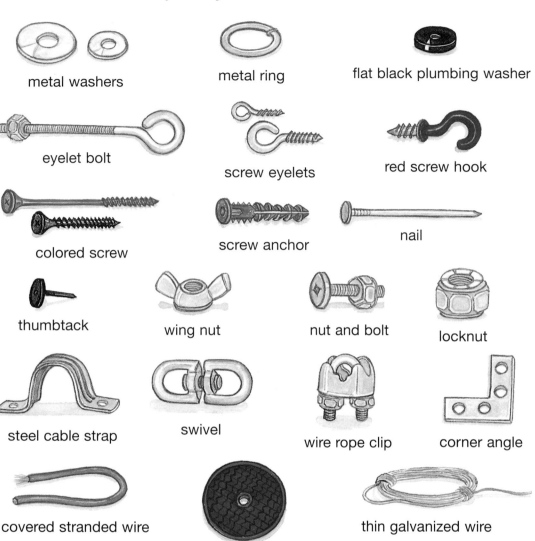

metal washers

metal ring

flat black plumbing washer

eyelet bolt

screw eyelets

red screw hook

colored screw

screw anchor

nail

thumbtack

wing nut

nut and bolt

locknut

steel cable strap

swivel

wire rope clip

corner angle

covered stranded wire

reflector

thin galvanized wire

adhesive automotive or safety tape

electrical tape

Safety notes

★ Wear gloves and safety glasses when you work with tools.

★ Ask an adult for help when trying something new or when using a glue gun, strong glue and an X-Acto knife.

Techniques

All of the projects in this book can be made in an afternoon. The skills you need are easy to learn, but read this section before you start. Make sure you ask an adult for help when it's suggested or when you are trying something new or difficult.

Safety

Wear safety glasses and work gloves to protect yourself, especially when working with wire.

Hand tools are safe when used carefully. Never force a tool, like a screwdriver — if it slips, it can hurt you. Ask an adult for help and take your time.

Work surface

Cover your work surface — a table or desk — with a large wooden board or thick piece of cardboard to protect it.

Substitutions

If you are missing some of the supplies, don't let that stop you! Use your imagination and use what you have. For example, instead of reflectors, try big buttons or washers. Instead of beads, try buttons or nuts. Instead of nylon fishing line, try dental floss. Instead of wire, try pipe cleaners. Nylon ribbon can be replaced by gift-wrapping ribbon. And if your wind chimes will be hanging indoors only, you can use cardboard or bristol board instead of plastic or acetate.

Plastic

Cut up old plastic or colored acetate report covers or even plastic lids or containers for your projects. Just be sure to use plastic that isn't so stiff that it cracks when folded.

Sometimes it's easier to fold plastic if you score it first. Draw a line on the plastic using a nail and ruler, and then make your fold along the line.

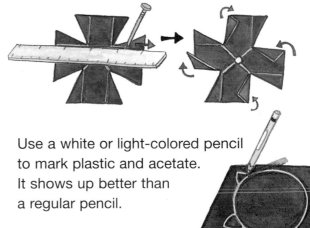

Use a white or light-colored pencil to mark plastic and acetate. It shows up better than a regular pencil.

Nylon fishing line

To hang your projects, use nylon fishing line. It is sold by the weight it can hold: 10 lb. line can hold a 10 lb. fish, 12 lb. line can hold a 12 lb. fish, and so on. For these projects, use 10 or 12 lb. line.

Fishing line is slippery, so knots can come untied. Make a big knot out of three or four smaller ones, then dab a bit of clear nail polish on the knot to stop it from coming undone.

To make a loop for hanging, fold over the fishing line about 5 cm (2 in.) from the end and tie a knot, as shown.

Tape

Automotive or safety tape has a backing that peels off. Electrical tape comes in rolls without a backing. If your tape is too wide, cut it down the center to make thinner strips.

To cut dots out of electrical tape, stick it to a strip of parchment or wax paper first. Use a hole punch to punch holes, then peel the dots off the paper.

Glue

Use a nontoxic waterproof or exterior glue for projects you'll hang outside. If you use a low-temperature glue gun, ask an adult to stand by or help. To glue metal, use a glue gun or ask an adult to use a strong glue recommended for metal.

Screwdrivers

Screwdrivers come in different sizes and types. Choose the one that fits tightly into the slot on the head of the screw or bolt.

Turn screw eyelets, screws, hooks, nuts and bolts clockwise (to the right) to tighten them and counterclockwise (to the left) to loosen them. Just remember: "righty-tighty, lefty-loosey."

Tips

• You won't be able to tell what something metal sounds like by holding and hitting it. It has to be free to vibrate, or shake. Try hanging the metal piece on a string and striking it with something else that's metal. Different-sized washers make different sounds. For example, bigger washers are louder and more musical.

• Use markers to color metal. If you paint metal, it won't ring in the wind anymore!

• Hang your wind chimes and whirligigs where you can see them and where they have room to move. Outside, mount them on a fence or hang them from a branch. You can also hang them outside or inside a window by the door. Indoors, hang wind chimes and whirligigs over (but not touching) a radiator or heating vent so the hot air makes them move.

• Make sure your wind chime or whirligig is attached well so that it doesn't fly away on a very windy day.

• If you find that the spot you chose is too windy or not windy enough, try another spot.

• If you want your wind chime to announce visitors, hang it above the door and tie on a long string with a bead at the end of it. When the door opens, it will catch the string and make the wind chime ring.

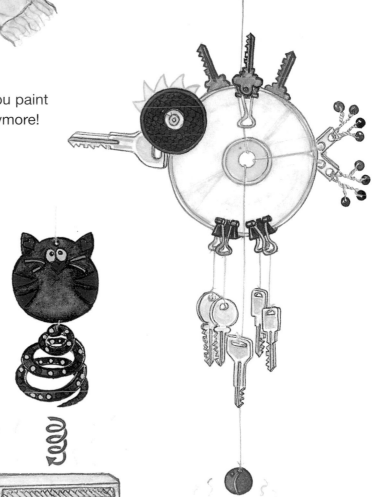

Crazy kitten

Watch it spin till it's dizzy — or you are.

You will need

- 10 cm x 25 cm (4 in. x 10 in.) piece of purple plastic
- small lid or jar, about 9 cm (3½ in.) diameter, for tracing around
- red and yellow safety tape
- permanent black marker
- scrap of green plastic
- nylon fishing line and nail polish
- white or light-colored pencil, scissors, hole punch, ruler

1 Place the lid on the purple plastic and trace around it. Repeat to make a second circle.

2 For the head, draw two pointy ears on one circle, about 4 cm (1½ in.) apart.

3 For the tail, draw a spiral in the other circle. Start at the outside edge and draw the lines about 1 cm (½ in.) apart, as shown.

4 Cut out both circles. Cut carefully around the ears of the first circle. Cut out the spiral of the second circle, starting at the edge.

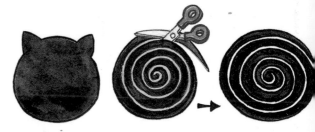

5 To decorate, cut triangles and hearts out of the red tape. Then cut two oval eyes out of the yellow tape and draw on the pupils with the marker. Using the hole punch, punch out red and yellow dots. Stick the decorations on the head and both sides of the tail.

6 Using the tip of your scissors, carefully poke tiny holes in the center of the tail and near the top and bottom of the head, as shown. Also poke two holes on each side of the nose.

7 For the whiskers, cut two very thin strips of green plastic about 8 cm (3 in.) long. From the back, poke the ends of the whiskers through the holes on either side of the nose, crisscrossed as shown.

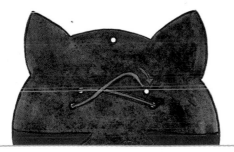

8 Make a double knot at the end of a 10 cm (4 in.) long piece of fishing line and slip the tail on. Tie on the tail so it hangs just below the head.

9 Tie a long piece of fishing line through the hole at the top of the head, as shown. Tie a loop at the other end for hanging. Dab nail polish on all the knots and cut off the ends.

Other idea

• Make a mad monkey instead.

Ring-a-ding bug

A real ding-a-linger to hang by the door to welcome visitors.

You will need

- $3/16$ in. wire rope clip
- 4 in. eyelet bolt
- two $3/16$ in. metal washers
- a yellow and a green pipe cleaner
- three $3/4$ in. colored binder clips
- 6 big metal washers in two or three different sizes
- green screw anchor
- nylon fishing line and nail polish
- scissors, ruler
- needlenose pliers

1 Unscrew the nuts on the wire rope clip and take it apart. Hook the U-bolt through the eyelet bolt.

2 Slip the rope clip back on the U-bolt. Then slip on the $3/16$ in. washers and screw the nuts back on loosely.

3 Twist the two pipe cleaners together.

4 For the nose and antennae, bend the striped pipe cleaner in half and poke it into the space between the rope clip and the eyelet bolt, as shown. Tighten the nuts with the pliers so the rope clip (the head) doesn't move.

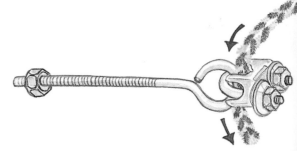

5 Curl the antennae and bend the nose down.

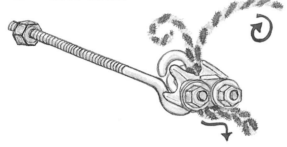

6 For the body, clip the binder clips to the eyelet bolt. Screw the screw anchor onto the end.

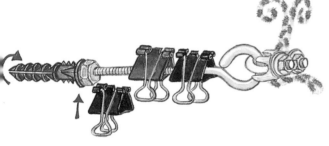

7 Tie a 20 cm (8 in.) piece of fishing line onto each washer. Use the line to tie a washer to each clip handle so three washers hang in a row and the other three hang in a lower row, as shown.

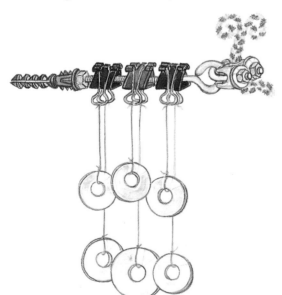

8 To hang the bug, tie a 45 cm (18 in.) piece of fishing line to both ends of the eyelet bolt, as shown. Tie a loop near the center of the line so your bug hangs straight. Dab nail polish on all the knots and cut off the ends.

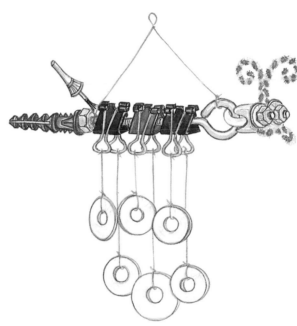

Other idea

• Make a not-so-noisy bug by using just three washers.

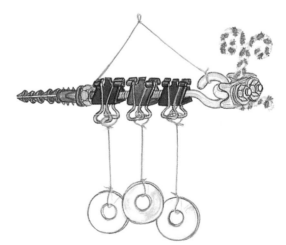

Clothespin fly

On sunny days, this fly will fill your room with rainbows.

You will need

- 3 different-colored acetate or plastic sheets
- colored electrical tape
- large plastic or wooden clothespin
- 2 black pipe cleaners
- 2 wooden beads about 1 cm (1/2 in.) diameter
- permanent black marker
- nylon fishing line and nail polish
- scissors, ruler

1 For the wings, cut a 3 cm x 15 cm (1¼ in. x 6 in.) strip from each acetate sheet. Round off the corners of the strips.

2 Pinch the wings together in the center to make a fold, as shown.

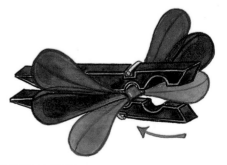

3 Place the wings on top of one another, with the middle one facing the opposite way. Tape them together, as shown.

4 Pinch the clothespin open and slide the wings in as far back as possible.

5 For the stinger, bend a pipe cleaner in half. Poke the ends up through the clothespin hole on either side, as shown. Twist the pipe cleaner together on the top of the clothespin to hold it closed.

6 Continue twisting the pipe cleaner ends together. Curl the stinger under.

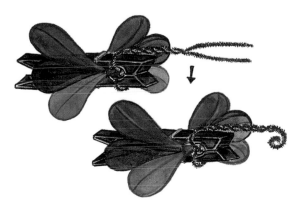

7 For the eyes and antennae, poke the other pipe cleaner through the clothespin spring so the pipe cleaner is the same length on each side. Twist the pipe cleaner together a few times to hold it in place.

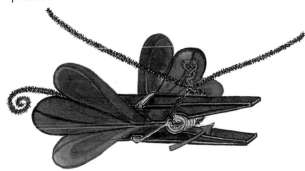

8 Slip a bead onto each end of the pipe cleaner until the beads touch the clothespin. Twist the pipe cleaners together a few times to hold the beads in place. Curl the ends. Draw pupils on the beads with the marker.

9 Tie a piece of fishing line around the clothespin so your fly hangs straight. Tie a loop at the other end of the string. Dab nail polish on the knots and cut off the ends.

Other ideas

Make different flies by
- having only one or two wings
- adding dots and stripes, bells or beads

15

Caterpillar

This 10-footed fellow sings softly in the breeze.

You will need

- old wooden spoon
- green, blue and black permanent markers
- 2 large natural wooden beads and one small red bead
- 5 cm (2 in.) square of green plastic

- tiny screw eyelet
- 10 long blue screws
- exterior wood glue or glue gun
- nylon fishing line and nail polish
- white or light-colored pencil, scissors, ruler, thumbtack

1 For the body, color blue and green stripes on the wooden spoon with the markers. For the eyes, color the large wooden beads green with a black pupil.

2 Glue the eyes and nose (the small red bead) onto the spoon. Let dry.

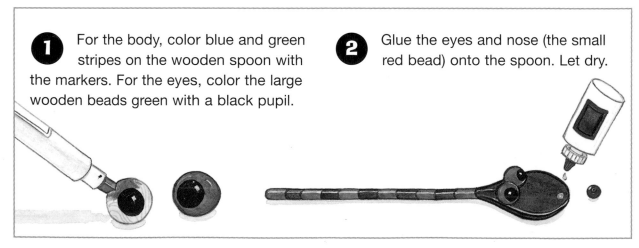

3 To make the spinner, draw two diagonal lines across the plastic square from corner to corner. Use the thumbtack to poke a small hole in the center where the lines cross.

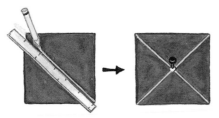

4 At each corner, draw a line about 2 cm (3/4 in.) long on either side of the diagonal lines, as shown. Cut along the lines.

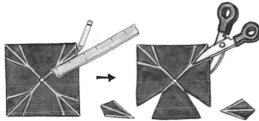

5 For each of the four sections, bend one corner up and the other corner down, as shown. (See page 7 for tips.)

6 Poke the screw eyelet through the hole in the center of the spinner and screw it into the flat end of the wooden spoon's handle. Blow on the spinner to check that it spins easily. Unscrew the eyelet a bit if it doesn't spin well.

7 Tie a 15 cm (6 in.) length of fishing line to the top of each screw. Tie the screws along the caterpillar's body in pairs, as shown.

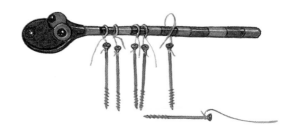

8 To hang, tie one end of a 50 cm (20 in.) length of fishing line to the neck of the body. Tie the other end about 5 cm (2 in.) from the spinner. Hang the caterpillar on a pencil so it hangs straight, and make a loop at that point. Dab nail polish on all the knots and cut off the ends.

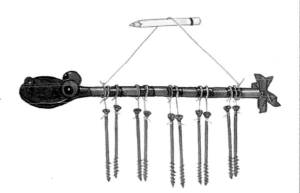

Other ideas

• Instead of screws, use old keys or other musical hardware pieces.

• Use a spatula, a spaghetti spoon or another utensil with a long handle instead of the wooden spoon.

Flutterfly

Watch this flit and flutter by in the wind.

You will need

- $3/16$ in. wire rope clip
- $3/8$ in. swivel
- two $1/4$ in. flat black plumbing washers
- 30 cm (12 in.) of green covered stranded wire
- 21 cm ($8^1/2$ in.) square of blue plastic
- red and yellow safety tape
- nylon fishing line and nail polish
- hole punch, ruler, nail (for scoring)
- needlenose pliers, X-Acto knife (optional)

1 Unscrew the nuts on the wire rope clip and take it apart. Hook the U-bolt onto one half of the swivel.

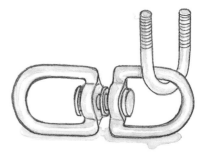

2 Slip the rope clip back on the U-bolt. Then slip on the black washers and screw the nuts back on loosely. (If the washer holes are too small, ask an adult to make them bigger by carefully using an X-Acto knife.)

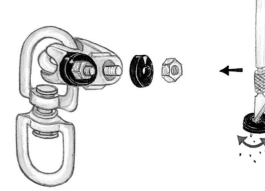

3 For the antennae, bend the green wire in half and poke it into the space between the rope clip and the swivel.

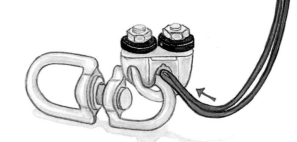

4 Tighten the nuts with the pliers so the rope clip (the head) doesn't move. Curl the antennae ends.

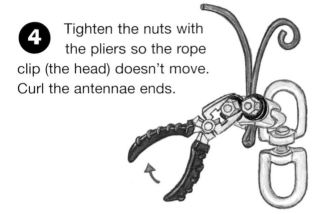

5 Pleat the plastic square as if you are making a fan. Make a 1.5 cm (³/₄ in.) fold along one edge, then flip the sheet over and make another fold the same width. Continue folding and flipping until you reach the other edge. You may need to score both sides of the plastic first (see page 7).

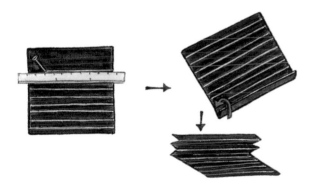

6 Keeping the plastic folded, slip it halfway through the bottom half of the swivel. Open the folds to make a fan on either side of the swivel.

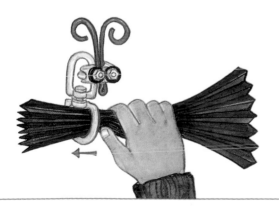

7 Punch lots of dots out of the red and yellow tape. Decorate both sides of the wings with the dots. Stick yellow dots on the end of the U-bolts for eyes.

8 Tie a long piece of fishing line to the head so the flutterfly hangs straight. Tie a loop at the other end of the line. Dab nail polish on the knots and cut off the ends.

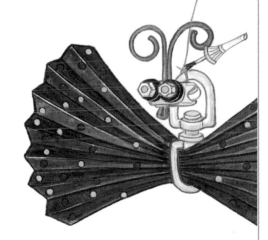

Other idea

• Tie on tiny bells to make a tinkerfly.

Crested key bird

CD birds get all keyed up when it's windy.

You will need

- 2 old CDs
- 3 metallic colored binder clips
- 7.5 cm (3 in.) square of yellow plastic
- 2 red reflectors, 6 cm (2½ in.) in diameter, with a hole in the middle
- 1 in. long ¼ in. bolt and nut
- two 5/16 in. metal washers
- 9 old keys
- corner angle
- 4 pieces of thin galvanized wire, 12 cm (4½ in.)
- 8 colored beads
- glue gun or strong glue
- nylon fishing line and nail polish
- colored pencil, scissors, ruler, permanent markers
- screwdriver
- safety glasses and work gloves

Tips

- If you can't find reflectors with holes, just glue on the washers in step 3.
- Have an adult help you while you glue.

1 For the body, clip the two CDs together, shiny side out, using two binder clips on one edge and one on the opposite edge, as shown.

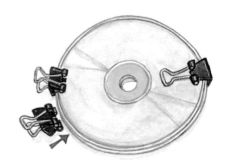

2 For the eyelashes, place a reflector half on the plastic. Trace around it and then draw points around the curve, as shown. Cut it out.

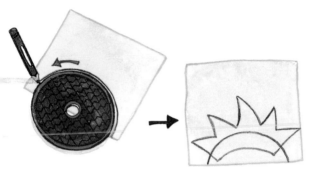

3 For the eyes, slip a washer on the bolt, then poke the bolt through the two reflectors. Slip on the other washer and screw the nut on loosely.

4 Slide the eyes onto the CDs. Trace around them on both sides and remove.

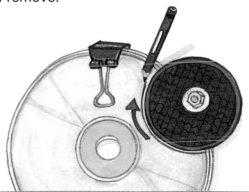

5 Carefully spread glue on the CDs inside the pencil line. Slide the reflector eyes back on and tighten the nut. Wipe off the excess glue and let dry.

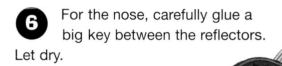

6 For the nose, carefully glue a big key between the reflectors. Let dry.

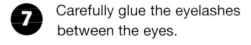

7 Carefully glue the eyelashes between the eyes.

8 For the crest, color three keys with the markers. Glue one key to the top clip and two to the CD body, one on each side of the clip. Let dry.

9 For the tail, bend the wires in half. Hook a wire through a hole in the end of the corner angle. Twist the wire to hold it in place. Repeat with the other three wires so there are two twisted wires at each end.

10 Slip a bead onto the ends of each piece of wire. Bend the wire back and twist it around to hold the bead in place.

11 Carefully glue the tail between the CDs. Let dry. For extra strength, tie the tail to the CDs with fishing line.

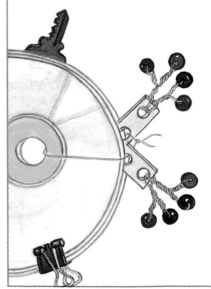

12 Tie a 15 cm (6 in.) piece of fishing line to four of the keys. Tie a key to each of the bottom clip handles. Tie a 30 cm (12 in.) line to the last key. Tie it to the CDs so it hangs between the other keys.

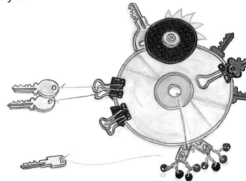

13 To hang, tie a piece of fishing line through the center hole of the CD. Tie a loop at the other end of the line. Dab nail polish on all the knots and cut off the ends.

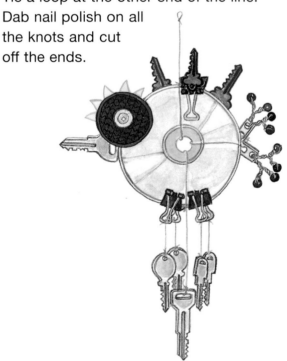

14 Hang your Crested Key Bird indoors near a window or outside in a sheltered spot.

Whirli-bug

This bug has a ball on windy days.

You will need

- tennis ball
- red screw hook
- three 1¹/₂ in. black screws
- two ⁵/₁₆ in. metal washers
- blue plastic, about 3 cm (1¹/₄ in.) square
- 3 blue plastic strips: 3 cm x 8 cm (1¹/₄ in. x 3¹/₄ in.)
- 1¹/₈ in. screw eyelet
- three ³/₁₆ metal washers
- safety or electrical tape
- nylon fishing line and nail polish
- scissors, ruler, hole punch, stapler
- screwdriver, work gloves, X-Acto knife (optional)

Tips

- If you are having trouble screwing things into the ball, ask an adult to make a small starter hole by carefully twirling the tip of the X-Acto knife at the right spot.
- Have a helper wearing work gloves hold the ball while you screw things into it.

1 For the nose, screw the red hook into one side of the ball.

2 For the eyes, slip a ⁵/₁₆ in. washer onto a black screw. Screw an eye on either side of the nose.

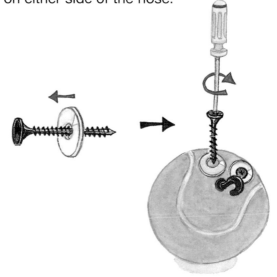

3 For the stinger, screw a black screw halfway into the ball on the opposite side of the nose.

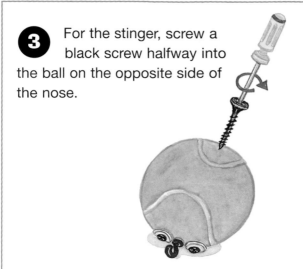

4 Cut a circle about 3 cm (1 1/4 in.) in diameter out of the square of plastic.

5 Punch a hole in the center of the circle.

6 For the propeller blades, round the corners off one end of each plastic strip with scissors, as shown.

7 Pinch together the square ends of the blades to make a fold, as shown.

8 Cut a 1 cm (1/2 in.) slit along the fold of each blade.

9 Pinch each blade together again. Hold them together with a thin strip of tape beside the slit, as shown.

10 For the propeller, slide a blade onto the circle. Use thin strips of tape and staples to hold it in place.

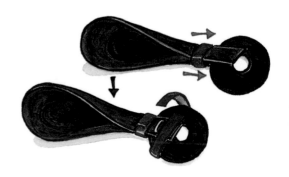

11 Tape and staple the other two blades to the circle. Make sure they all face the same direction.

12 Slip a 3/16 in. washer, the propeller and the two other washers on the screw eyelet.

13 Screw the propeller into the top of the ball, as shown. Blow on it to check that it spins easily. Unscrew the eyelet a bit if it doesn't spin well.

14 To hang, tie a piece of fishing line to the screw eyelet. Tie a loop at the other end of the line. Dab nail polish on the knots and cut off the ends.

Other idea

• Make a whirli-ladybug by using a pink tennis ball and pushing in black thumbtacks for the spots.

Racing snails

Who will catch the wind?

You will need

- green oil pastel crayons and tissues
- wooden board about 40 cm (16 in.) long
- 3 locknuts: two $5/8$ in. and one $1/2$ in.
- yellow safety tape
- 3 steel cable straps: two 2 in. and one 1 in.
- three $5/16$ in. metal washers
- three $5/16$ in. wing nuts
- three $1\frac{1}{2}$ in. black screws
- three $1\frac{1}{8}$ in. screw eyelets
- screwdriver
- three $9/16$ in. metal washers
- big gold metal bell
- aluminum pie plate
- black, red and blue permanent markers
- nylon fishing line and nail polish
- scissors, hole punch

For the snails

1 Color the wooden board with green pastels and rub it with a tissue.

2 For the eyes, punch six dots out of the yellow tape and stick two on each nut. Draw on black pupils.

3 Arrange the cable straps (the snail bodies) on the board at different angles. For each head, stack a nut, a $5/16$ in. washer and a wing nut on one end.

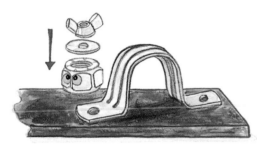

4 Screw each head into the board with a black screw. Screw in each tail end with a screw eyelet.

For the moving parts

1 Color one side of the $9/16$ in. washers with the red marker. Tie a piece of fishing line around each.

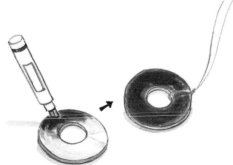

2 Tie one washer to the top of a large snail's back so it hangs in the middle. Tie the other washers to hang on either side.

3 Tie the bell inside the small snail.

4 Cut a 4.5 cm ($1^3/4$ in.) circle from the pie plate. Color one side with the blue marker. Punch holes on opposite edges of the circle. Thread a piece of fishing line through the holes and tie the ends to the sides of the last snail.

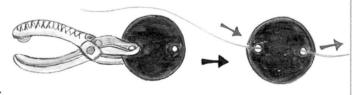

5 Dab nail polish on all the knots and cut off the ends. Dab some on the fishing line where it's tied to the snail.

Spiderweb

Catch some sunshine instead of flies.

You will need

- metal coat hanger
- 20 gauge galvanized wire: five 35 cm (14 in.) lengths and five 50 cm (20 in.) lengths
- small sparkling beads (optional)
- nylon fishing line and nail polish
- 2 black pipe cleaners
- bottle cap
- 2 small wooden beads
- small golden bells
- ruler, scissors
- needlenose pliers, glue gun
- safety glasses and work gloves

1 For the frame, bend the coat hanger into a circle. Use the pliers to shape it.

2 Bend the hook into a loop using the pliers, as shown. Wind a 35 cm (14 in.) piece of wire around the loop ends to hold it in place.

3 For the spokes of the web, wind one end of a piece of 35 cm (14 in.) wire a few times around the coat hanger near the top, as shown. Wind the other end around the opposite side of the circle.

4 Repeat step 3 with the other three wires, starting at different points around the circle, as shown. Make sure the wires cross in the center.

5 For the web, start at the center and wind a piece of 50 cm (20 in.) wire around the spokes. Making an outward spiral, wrap the wire once around each spoke as you come to it. When you run out of wire, hook another wire to the end of the last wire. Continue the spiral until you reach the frame.

6 If you want, tie one end of a 45 cm (18 in.) length of fishing line to the frame between two spokes. Thread some sparkling beads onto the line and loop the line around the wire spiral. Continue threading and looping until you reach the opposite side. Tie the end to the frame. Repeat between the other spokes.

7 To make the spider's legs, cut the pipe cleaners in half and fold the ends under.

8 Carefully glue the legs to the inside of the bottle cap and let dry. Glue the wooden beads to the top of the cap for eyes and let dry.

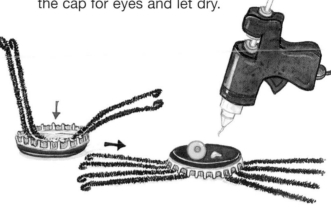

9 Bend the legs up near the bottle cap and then down again at the middle, as shown.

10 Tie the spider to the web with fishing line. Tie on a few bells to hang around the web. Dab nail polish on all the knots and cut off the ends.

Big fish, little fish

When the wind blows, these fish really go.

You will need

- 20 cm (8 in.) square of light blue plastic
- plate, about 20 cm (8 in.) diameter
- 5 cm (2 in.) square of green plastic
- 4 cm (1½ in.) square of dark blue plastic
- red and yellow safety tape
- 12.5 cm (5 in.) square of dark blue plastic
- straightened wire hanger or stiff wire cut into two lengths: 30 cm (12 in.) and 50 cm (20 in.)
- 10 small wooden beads that fit snugly on the wire
- permanent black marker
- nylon fishing line and nail polish
- white or light-colored pencil, scissors, hole punch, ruler, thumbtack, a quarter
- wire cutters, exterior glue or glue gun

1 To make the big fish, place the plate on the light blue plastic and trace around it. Cut out the circle.

2 Draw a round mouth about 6 cm (2½ in.) wide. Cut it out.

3 Punch two holes beside the mouth, about 1 cm (½ in.) apart. Punch two more holes on the opposite edge of the circle.

4 Punch one hole near the top of the circle and one near the bottom.

5 For the fins, cut two triangles, about 5 cm (2 in.) high, out of the plastic left over from step 1.

6 With a thumbtack, poke holes about 2.5 cm (1 in.) from either side of the bottom hole of the big fish. Poke a hole near a corner on each fin.

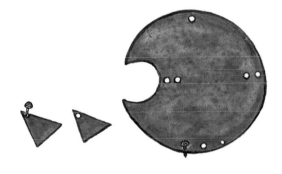

7 Using fishing line, tie on the fins so they hang just below the fish.

8 For the little fish, cut a 5 cm (2 in.) circle out of the green plastic. Draw a little round mouth and cut it out. Punch a hole beside the mouth and one on the opposite edge of the circle.

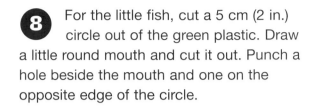

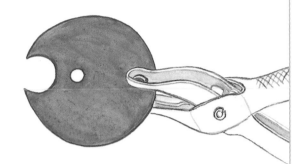

9 To make a spinner tail for the little fish, use the small dark blue square of plastic and follow steps 3 to 5 of the Caterpillar instructions (see page 17).

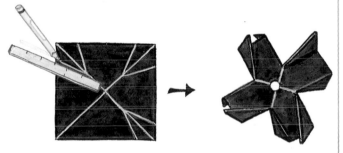

10 Decorate both sides of the little fish and the big fish with dots, squiggles and big eyes cut from the safety tape. Draw pupils on the eyes with the black marker.

31

11 To make the pinwheel tail for the big fish, draw lines from corner to corner to make an X on the big dark blue square of plastic.

12 Cut along the lines, up to about 2.5 cm (1 in.) from the center.

13 Punch a hole in the center. Punch a hole in the same corner of each triangle, as shown.

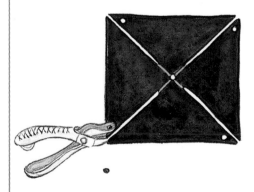

14 Make four circles on the red tape by tracing around a quarter. Cut out the circles. Punch holes in the center of the circles.

15 Curve the tips of the triangles into the center, lining up the holes. Bend the triangles gently so they stay curved.

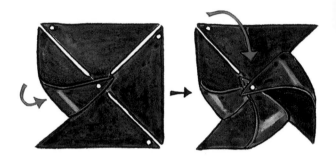

16 Stick two of the tips together between two red circles, carefully lining up all the holes. Stick a third triangle tip in place with another circle. Repeat for the last triangle tip.

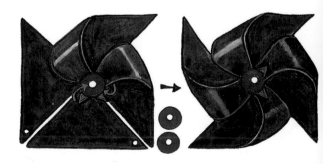

17 Glue a bead to one end of each wire. Let dry.

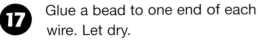

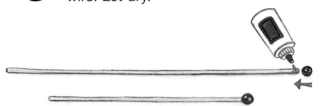

20 Finally, slide on the little fish and glue a bead to the end of the wire. Let dry.

18 To assemble the fish, first slide the pinwheel onto the shorter wire until it touches the bead. Slip on another bead to hold the pinwheel in place. Check that the pinwheel spins easily by blowing on it. Glue the bead in place and let dry.

21 Poke the long wire through the top and bottom holes on the big fish. Glue a bead on the wire just below the fish to stop it from sliding down.

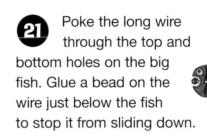

19 Next, poke the wire through the double holes on the big fish. Slip on and glue four red beads (in the mouth). Then slide on the little fish's spinner tail and a bead to hold it in place. Check that the spinner turns, then glue on the bead.

22 Stick the fish in the ground or in a big flowerpot. Or have an adult attach it to a railing using fence staples.

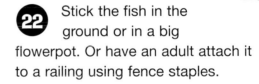

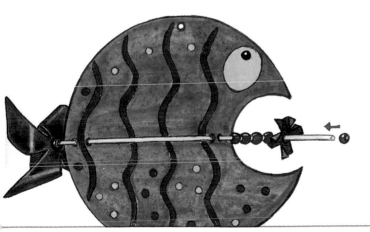

Wind dragon

This dragon dances up a storm in windy weather.

- metal coat hanger
- small metal ring
- old metal fork
- red and white safety or electrical tape
- 2 table tennis balls
- 45 cm (18 in.) length of thin galvanized wire
- clean, empty, green plastic soft drink bottle
- yellow, red and blue nylon ribbon
- strong nylon fishing line and nail polish
- piece of red plastic, 9 cm x 25 cm (3½ in. x 10 in.)
- 1 piece of blue plastic and 2 pieces of yellow plastic, 15 cm x 28 cm (6 in. x 11 in.)
- red, green and black permanent markers
- white or light-colored pencil, ruler, scissors, hole punch, thumbtack
- wire cutter, needlenose pliers
- work gloves and safety glasses

1 Turn the hook of the coat hanger to face you, and slip on the metal ring. Then ask an adult to cut off the bottom of the hanger at the corners.

2 Bend the handle of the fork with pliers so it has about the same curve as the coat hanger hook. Tape the fork to the top of the hook, as shown. Color the handle of the fork red.

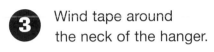

3 Wind tape around the neck of the hanger.

4 Draw eyes on the table tennis balls with the markers. With a thumbtack, gently poke small holes on opposite sides of both balls, as shown.

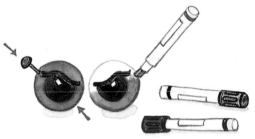

5 To attach the eyes, wrap the middle of the wire twice around the tape holding the fork and hanger together. Twist the wire a few times.

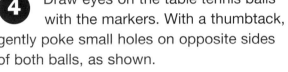

6 Poke a wire end through the holes in each ball. Twist the two wires together to hold the eyeballs together. Wrap the wires back down around the fork to hold the eyes in place.

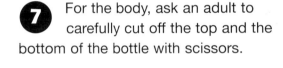

7 For the body, ask an adult to carefully cut off the top and the bottom of the bottle with scissors.

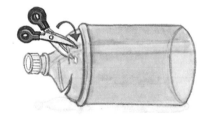

8 Punch four evenly spaced holes around the large end. Punch eight evenly spaced holes all around the small end.

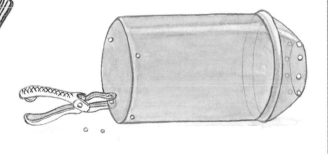

9 For the tail, cut different lengths of yellow, red and blue ribbon. Cut the strips down the center to make them thinner. Knot them two at a time to the small end of the bottle, as shown.

10 Cut two blue and two red 45 cm (18 in.) strips of ribbon. Cut them down the center. Tie two to each hole around the large end of the bottle, as shown.

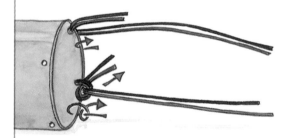

11 Knot all the ribbons from step 10 together, then tie them to the metal ring, as shown. Tie a piece of fishing line from each hole to the ring for extra strength.

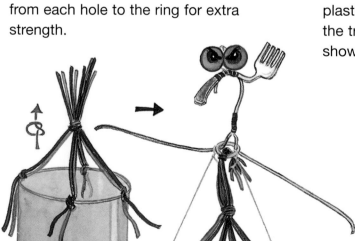

12 For the mouth, fold the red piece of plastic in half. Unfold it and draw a triangle on each half, as shown.

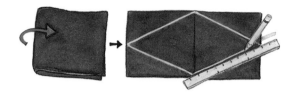

13 Draw a few small triangles along each edge for teeth.

14 Cut out the mouth. Cut a small slit (to fit the end of the fork) in the middle of the center fold.

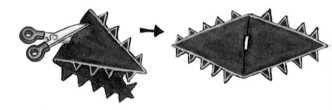

15 For the head crest and the wings, use the blue and yellow pieces of plastic. Trace around the mouth, but make the triangles along each edge bigger, as shown. Cut them out.

16 Stick white tape on the teeth and trim off the excess. Bend them in.

17 Fold the mouth and slip it onto the fork. Wind tape around the handle of the fork to hold the mouth in place.

18 Pinch the middle of the blue head crest together and slide it under the middle two prongs of the fork.

19 Punch two holes in each yellow wing, one near each end. Then cut a small slit in the center.

20 Bend the coat hanger arms back a bit and slip on the wings. Wind tape around the ends and middle of the hanger to hold the wings in place.

21 To hang, tie one end of a long piece of fishing line around the fork so the dragon hangs straight. Tie a loop at the other end of the line. Dab nail polish on all the knots and cut off the ends.

Other idea

• Make a peacock with a fan-shaped head crest and less pointy wings.

Whirli-bird

Watch the wind whisk and whirl this rooster around.

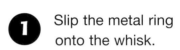

You will need

- old kitchen whisk
- 1 in. metal ring
- $1/4$ in. dowel, 23 cm (9 in.) long
- old metal tablespoon
- $1/4$ in. wire rope clip
- two $5/16$ in. metal washers
- 10 cm x 23 cm (4 in. x 9 in.) piece of red plastic
- red and yellow safety or electrical tape
- 23 cm x 15 cm (9 in. x 6 in.) piece of black plastic
- yellow and red nylon ribbon
- nylon fishing line and nail polish
- white or light-colored pencil, ruler, scissors, hole punch, black permanent marker
- needlenose pliers
- exterior glue and toothpick or glue gun

1 Slip the metal ring onto the whisk.

2 Color the dowel black with the marker. Stick the dowel through the whisk just above the ring, as shown.

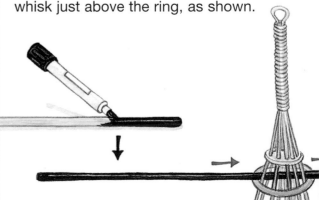

3 For the beak, hold the spoon near the neck with the pliers and bend the handle up, as shown.

4 Tape the spoon onto the whisk handle.

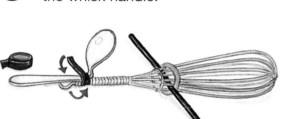

5 For the eyes, unscrew the nuts on the wire rope clip and take it apart. Hook the U-bolt on the whisk handle where the spoon is taped on.

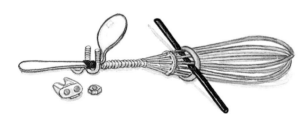

6 Slip the rope clip back on the U-bolt. Slip on the washers and screw the nuts back on loosely.

7 Use a toothpick to dab a bit of glue on the threads of the U-bolt, as shown. Screw the nuts back on tightly with the pliers. Let dry.

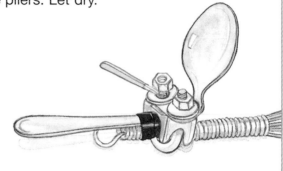

8 To make the head comb, draw a line across one long side of the red plastic, about 2.5 cm (1 in.) from the edge. Make cuts up to the line every .5 cm (¼ in.), as shown.

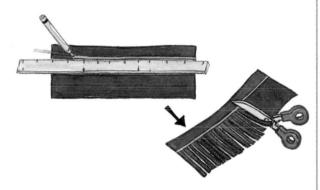

9 Wind the comb around the top of the handle and hold it together with two thin strips of yellow tape.

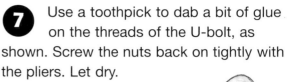

10 Bend the strips gently to curl them.

11 Draw two wing shapes on the black plastic and cut them out. Punch two holes in each wing, as shown.

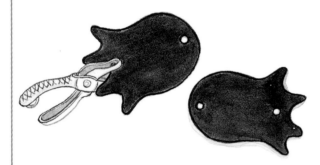

12 Punch lots of dots out of the red and yellow tape. Stick them to both sides of the wings and comb and to the beak and eyes.

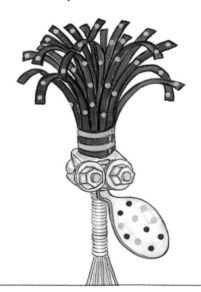

13 Poke the dowel through the holes in the wings so they curve in opposite directions, as shown. Wind thin strips of tape around the ends of the dowel so the wings don't slip off.

14 For the tail, cut different lengths of nylon ribbon. Cut them down the center to make them thinner. Knot them to the bottom of the whisk.

15 To hang, tie a piece of fishing line to the top of the whisk. Tie a loop at the other end. Dab nail polish on the knots and cut off the ends.